THE ASSERTIVENESS POCKETBOOK

D1152006

By Max A. Eggert

Drawings by Phil Hailstone

Dedication

This book is dedicated to my son, Max Charles, who, in spite of my influence, is very much his own man and, for one so young, has developed his own way of being assertive. Max, I'm proud of you.

Thanks to Donna Coiera for transforming my handwriting into an acceptable WP format.

"Will appeal to anyone in human resources or management training. It is successful in keeping jargon to a minimum without loss of precision. The concepts are immediately relevant, and each page will offer you a new idea, a new skill or a new way to look at a situation."
Louise Campbell, Associate Director, Human Resources, Societe Generale Australia Ltd.

"This pocketbook provides at a glance the skills required for a lifetime."
Tracey Luscombe, Human Resource Manager, Manchester Unity Friendly Society in NSW.

CONTENTS

INTRODUCTION

DEFINITION OF ASSERTIVENESS

Assertive: (adj) confident and direct in dealing with others.
Collins Concise English Dictionary

Assertiveness is upholding one's own integrity and dignity whilst at the same time encouraging and recognising this behaviour in others.

INCREASING POPULARITY

Assertiveness and the skills associated with it are increasing in popularity because:

- There has been an increase in individual freedom

- It empowers people who use it

- It encourages psychological health in those who use it

- In less hierarchical work structures, managing by rank alone is no longer effective

- More competition for resources makes it necessary for individuals to pursue what they want

WITH WHOM CAN YOU BE ASSERTIVE?

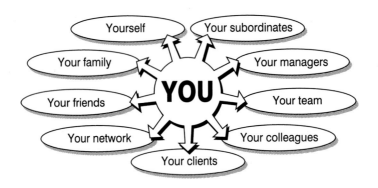

In fact, assertiveness is useful for everyone with whom you come into contact.

INTRODUCTION

WHY ASSERTIVENESS NOW?

- Social and political hierarchies based on birth or caste are no longer successful within capitalist structures

- Successful enterprises are based on meritocracy and need everyone to achieve their best

- To be successful, society requires all to make a contribution - no one person is inherently better than another

- To speak one's mind and to reveal one's true position have been found to engender psychological health and improved relationships

- At work the person doing the job is the one who can make the most significant contribution to improvements on the job

- The political value and power behind the equality movement for gender, race, religion, colour and ethnic origin are now integrated into the culture of western civilisation

- The full fruition of democratic principles of individual freedom, and the equal rights of all within society, encourage all to pursue their rights and aims

- The New Age philosophy of individual empowerment and pursuit of personal excellence encourages people to be themselves

WHEN TO USE ASSERTIVENESS

ASSERTIVENESS AND INTEGRITY

When we are assertive we increase our integrity because we are honest with ourselves and with others.

WITH SELF	HONESTY	WITH OTHERS
What you feel		Their impact on you
What you think		Their behaviour
What you need		What you want from them

When we are honest with ourselves and with others we are able to achieve what we want without compromise.

KEEPING A BALANCE

In assertiveness we balance the needs of others with our own. We treat others as we wish to be treated. When necessary we can choose whether to give priority to the needs of others or choose to give greater consideration to our own needs.

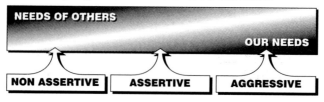

WEAK : When we put all the needs of others before our own

AGGRESSIVE : When we put personal needs before those of others

ASSERTIVE : When we balance our needs and those of others and act according to the priorities as we see them

THREE BEHAVIOUR TYPES

THREE BEHAVIOUR TYPES

THE THREE OPTIONS

When faced with difficult situations animals have two options:

FLIGHT = non-assertion
FIGHT = aggression.

Humankind has a third option: ASSERTIVENESS, which is essentially a considered response to difficult situations.

Let us look at these three options:

- Non-assertion
- Aggression
- Assertiveness

so that we can recognise them in ourselves and be able to manage them constructively.

THREE BEHAVIOUR TYPES

1. NON-ASSERTIVE BEHAVIOUR

The non-assertive person:

- Is reluctant to express own opinions, and particularly, feelings
- Often feels used by others
- Keeps quiet when others take advantage
- Refrains from complaining when services or products are not up to standard
- Finds it difficult to refuse the requests of others for time or resources
- Acquiesces in the views and desires of the majority even though these conflict with personal wishes
- Frequently makes compromises in the interests of harmony
- Is unwilling to inconvenience people for the things he or she wants
- Is submissive in the presence of aggressive behaviour
- Prefers to keep own views private

11

THREE BEHAVIOUR TYPES

1. NON-ASSERTIVE BEHAVIOUR

OUR REASONS

Fear of upsetting others

There is a myth in interpersonal relations that goes like this. *If you sacrifice enough, work hard enough, care enough, forgive enough, other people will give you their approval.*
It gets worse. *If you don't gain their approval it is because you are not giving up enough, working hard enough, caring enough, etc.*

- You can choose to change your behaviour if you think that the cost of losing someone's friendship is higher than doing or saying what you want; but it is indeed rare for anything to be that significant

- What you are is something absolute, and independent of the goodwill of others; **what others think of you does not make you any more or any less of what you are**

- People usually want you to change your behaviour when they don't get exactly what they want; even if they think ill of you, what you know yourself to be does not change

1. NON-ASSERTIVE BEHAVIOUR

OUR REASONS

Fear of rejection

This is the extreme version of fear of upsetting others. If we upset someone by asking for what we want, we fear they will withdraw their regard for us and reject us altogether.

- In any relationship there has to be give and take, but if it is all 'take', then the relationship is essentially flawed at a basic level, and the price is too high for any individual to pay

- Usually, a moment's reflection is enough to make you realise that:
  a) if they say no, they are unlikely to reject you personally, and
  b) if they do want to reject you then the price of their friendship is too high anyway

THREE BEHAVIOUR TYPES

1. NON-ASSERTIVE BEHAVIOUR

OUR REASONS

Feeling responsible for the other person

There is a real difference between hurting someone and someone feeling hurt. You are not responsible for their feelings; if they 'feel' hurt because of a reasonable need that you have, then that is their choice.

This is totally different from a situation where, through aggressive behaviour, you hurt someone by abusing their rights, taking deliberate advantage or by not respecting them as a person.

Inappropriate inner voices

This occurs when the rules by which we live have been determined by others, usually during childhood, and we still operate by them. (See page 22 for further thoughts on this.)

1. NON-ASSERTIVE BEHAVIOUR

SELF-DEFEATING MIND GAMES

Someone once said that there are two realities - the way we think things are, and the way they really are. The way we think about ourselves and our experience can very much affect us and our behaviour. If our perceptions are our reality we must be very careful not to play self-defeating mind games. We must be aware of what psychologists call 'cognitive distortions', that is the way the mind lays an inappropriate explanation over a neutral experience.

NEUTRAL FACTS + EMOTIONAL INTERPRETATION = DISTORTED REALITY

Here are the more common games
we play to defeat ourselves:

- **G** GENERALISATION
- **D** DOOMSDAYING
- **L** LABELLING
- **MR** MIND READING
- **F** FILTERING
- **P** PERSONALISING

We examine them in turn.

1. **NON-ASSERTIVE BEHAVIOUR**

SELF-DEFEATING MIND GAMES

G **Generalisation**

This is taking one event and thinking it will always occur.

'I failed once therefore I always fail', or
'I did not get it right first time so I will never get it right'.

This takes us back to 'if you think you can or you
think you can't, you're right'. You get what you expect.
Your life becomes a self-fulfilling prophecy of failure.
Most upsets in life are 'small stuff'.

D **Doomsdaying**

This is magnifying something, typically blowing up a small
failure out of all proportion, as if it will bring about the
end of the world. The normal ups and downs of
everyday life become a series of huge tragedies and
dramas which compound feelings of personal failure.

THREE BEHAVIOUR TYPES

1. NON-ASSERTIVE BEHAVIOUR

SELF-DEFEATING MIND GAMES

 Labelling

When you hang a large sign around your neck which says 'hopeless', or 'lazy' or 'friendless' then you are labelling yourself. When an opportunity occurs for you to do something, you look down at your label and act accordingly. Like Daffy Duck, if you have a label that says 'No one loves me' around your neck, and you keep saying it to yourself, it quickly becomes reality.

MR **Mind reading**

You smile at a friend at a party and they ignore you; immediately you think they don't like you or you have upset them. This is because you can read minds, and just by looking at them you can tell exactly what they think. The fact that they are short-sighted, or thinking hard about something, or even a little intoxicated is neither here nor there.

People do things for a whole host of reasons and it is self-defeating to 'mind read' into their behaviour a negative attitude towards yourself.

THREE BEHAVIOUR TYPES

1. NON-ASSERTIVE BEHAVIOUR

SELF-DEFEATING MIND GAMES

F Filtering

Filters do a great job of taking out unwanted material, but in the case of a personal filter it removes all the positive things that occur in your life. Rather like the reverse of rose-tinted glasses, people who filter only accept bad news about themselves and their situations. Thus confirming their view of the world.

P Personalising

When you personalise, you take full personal responsibility for a mishap or difficulty. Events occur for a whole host of reasons, but you take full personal responsibility even if your part was minor.

You can always do more, try harder, be more persistent, but you can't control or be the cause of everything. If you continually personalise the events in your life you will be condemned to a life of everlasting doubt, guilt, blame and self-denigration.

1. NON-ASSERTIVE BEHAVIOUR

THE TYRANNY CIRCLE OF MUSTS

Non-assertive persons are imprisoned by 'musts' in their head.

THREE BEHAVIOUR TYPES

1. NON-ASSERTIVE BEHAVIOUR

THE PRISON BARS OF INAPPROPRIATE OBLIGATION

Freedom and assertiveness are about choosing the rules you wish to live by.

THREE BEHAVIOUR TYPES

1. NON-ASSERTIVE BEHAVIOUR

SELF TALK: FAILURE AND SUCCESS

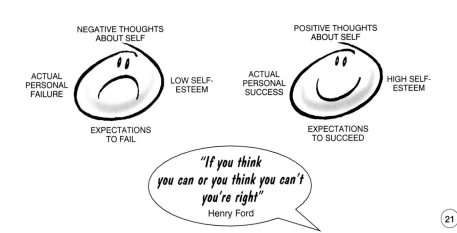

NEGATIVE THOUGHTS ABOUT SELF

ACTUAL PERSONAL FAILURE

LOW SELF-ESTEEM

EXPECTATIONS TO FAIL

POSITIVE THOUGHTS ABOUT SELF

ACTUAL PERSONAL SUCCESS

HIGH SELF-ESTEEM

EXPECTATIONS TO SUCCEED

"If you think you can or you think you can't you're right"
Henry Ford

THREE BEHAVIOUR TYPES

1. NON-ASSERTIVE BEHAVIOUR
THE TYRANNY OF INNER VOICES

Sometimes the way we talk to ourselves works against us. We all have voices in our heads that monitor what we do and how we behave. Sometimes the voices are our own; sometimes they are voices of people significant in our past: parents or teachers, in fact anyone in our childhood who was emotionally significant. Sometimes the voices are helpful, sometimes not. Whilst it may be difficult to stop the voices, even when you know it is your mother speaking, you can decide whether or not to be influenced. Here are some of the more inappropriate voices:

- Don't make a fuss
- Always respect your elders and betters
- You must always work hard
- Real men don't cry
- A good woman is always patient
- All's well that ends well
- Don't bring your problems home
- You must work harder

- Life is not supposed to be fun
- Be good
- Children should be seen and not heard
- Don't interrupt
- Grin and bear it
- Be perfect
- Finish what you start

THREE BEHAVIOUR TYPES

1. NON-ASSERTIVE BEHAVIOUR
THE TYRANNY OF INNER VOICES

When we first came into the world, we had no difficulty making our needs felt. We were also exceptionally flexible, doing whatever it took to get fed, or get attention. It was only later that we lost our spontaneity and internalised the 'shoulds' and 'oughts' of others.

To be assertive is to recognise that sometimes the inner voice is useful, and at other times it is restrictive and inappropriate. By all means listen to the inner voice, but do not allow yourself to be ruled by it at all times.

2. AGGRESSIVE BEHAVIOUR

The aggressive person:

- Frequently argues with others
- Frequently gets angry and thinks that others need to be put in their place
- Has no difficulty in complaining when receiving poor quality products or services
- Usually gets own way in situations
- Expects others to accommodate own time schedules
- Has strong views on many subjects and has no difficulty in expressing them
- Easily and frequently finds fault with others
- Continually works to personal agendas at the expense of others
- Rarely feels aware of the needs or feelings of others
- Competes with others and is angry if not successful

2. AGGRESSIVE BEHAVIOUR

AGGRESSION

Aggressive individuals are essentially selfish. They know what they want and like, and disregard the needs of others in satisfying their own needs.

Aggressive people think of themselves as superior beings. They think they are OK and the rest of the world is not. They voice their opinions and needs, and behave as if others do not matter.

The origin for aggressive behaviour is complex. Perhaps as small children aggressive people discovered they could get what they wanted, and subsequently developed behaviour around this inappropriate, albeit successful, behaviour. Sometimes aggressive behaviour is an over-correction of being too passive, or it could be an inappropriate way of dealing with anger.

3. ASSERTIVE BEHAVIOUR

The assertive person:

- Is able to express desires and feelings to others
- Is able to converse and work well with people at all levels
- Is able to appreciate the views of others and accept any that appear more reasonable than their own
- Is able to disagree with someone yet retain their friendship and respect
- Is aware of the needs and desires of others
- Is able to make concessions to others without feelings of inadequacy
- Is able to express a concern or a need with minimum embarrassment to both parties
- Is able to control feelings and emotions even in difficult or emotionally charged situations
- Is able to refuse a request without feeling guilty or obliged
- Is able to ask for what he or she wants and can insist on legal entitlements without becoming emotional

THREE BEHAVIOUR TYPES

3. ASSERTIVE BEHAVIOUR

DOUBLE ADVANTAGE

NON-ASSERTIVE		AGGRESSIVE	
DISADVANTAGES	**ADVANTAGES**	**ADVANTAGES**	**DISADVANTAGES**
Low self-esteem	You don't always have to win	High self-esteem	You get isolated
You don't state your views	You fit in easily	You get what you want	You are not popular
Feelings of anxiety	You don't feel guilty	You express your needs	You hurt others
You get put upon	You don't upset people	People don't take advantage	You take advantage

THE BENEFITS OF BEING ASSERTIVE

Assertiveness enjoys the advantages of non-assertion and aggressiveness and has none of the disadvantages of either.

3. ASSERTIVE BEHAVIOUR

PSYCHOLOGICAL ADVANTAGES

- You can put limits on your own behaviour and that of others

- You can enjoy a realistic outlook on what is possible for you and what is not

- You are not adversely affected by rude or impolite people

- You are able to rejoice at your successes and accept your failings

- You can always be in control of your own behaviour and not be pushed into a rage or forced into submission

3. ASSERTIVE BEHAVIOUR

THE LIBERATION OF INNER VOICES

Inner voices can be limiting, but they can also influence our behaviour positively. This being so, it is critical that we develop statements for ourselves that are strong and positive. If our self-perception can create our reality, then we must perceive ourselves in the right way. One way to do this is through the use of affirmations.

If you keep telling yourself you are something then that is the way your behaviour orientates itself. If you tell yourself you are successful and fortunate it changes your expectations of the world, and your interpretation of what you receive from it. This is a well established principle - all top athletes see themselves as successful and winning; it gives them that psychological edge. By using affirmations you can give yourself that same edge.

The liberation circle on the following page shows you how the positive affirmation 'I am assertive' works. Notice it is not how successful you are that counts, but how you behave. Behave according to your affirmation and success will follow.

THREE BEHAVIOUR TYPES

3. ASSERTIVE BEHAVIOUR

THE LIBERATION CIRCLE

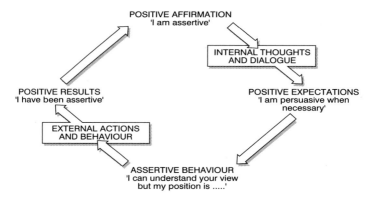

POSITIVE AFFIRMATION
'I am assertive'

INTERNAL THOUGHTS
AND DIALOGUE

POSITIVE RESULTS
'I have been assertive'

EXTERNAL ACTIONS
AND BEHAVIOUR

POSITIVE EXPECTATIONS
'I am persuasive when
necessary'

ASSERTIVE BEHAVIOUR
'I can understand your view
but my position is .....'

'The more you do of what you're doing the more you get of what you've got.'

THREE BEHAVIOUR TYPES

3. ASSERTIVE BEHAVIOUR

AFFIRMATIONS

Using affirmations is one way to improve our inner voices.

An affirmation is a personal statement which encapsulates beliefs about ourselves that we hold dear. Affirmations can be positive or negative. Obviously, positive affirmations are better for our mental well-being.

Positive affirmations help you:

- Cast off the limitations of other people's beliefs that you inherited during childhood
- Become your own person so you can stand alone and be strong
- Gain self-confidence

On the following page are some examples of affirmations, but give some thought to developing your own. Take time to read them regularly, especially first thing in the morning and last thing at night.

THREE BEHAVIOUR TYPES

3. ASSERTIVE BEHAVIOUR

AFFIRMATIONS FOR WORK

- I am a competent and confident person
- I always learn from my mistakes and those of others
- I am an attractive and interesting person
- People listen to what I have to say
- At meetings I make a significant contribution
- I am persuasive and influential
- I am responsible for myself and my actions
- I am independent of the approval of others
- I can always find opportunities in situations of change
- I am creating my desired future

Some of these affirmations may appeal, others may not. What is important is that you develop a set for yourself.

3. **ASSERTIVE BEHAVIOUR**

AFFIRMATIONS FOR LIFE

- I am what I am
- I have all the resources to do what I want to do
- I am at one with myself and my world
- I am free to be what I want to be
- I respect myself and all living things
- In being myself I express the godhead within me
- In loving myself I love others
- I am continually developing towards my inner self
- All things have meaning and there is always opportunity in adversity
- In giving I achieve more
- I am open to the opportunities this day brings

34

RIGHTS & RESPONSIBILITIES

BASIC RIGHTS

DEFINITION

Recognition that individuals living in a free society should enjoy entitlements which encourage them to behave in ways that empower them psychologically to become fully functional, to the benefit of themselves and society at large.

This means that you can:
- Behave according to your rights without needing permission or approval from others
- Expect to use these rights without being asked to justify your behaviour
- Encourage others to use these rights for themselves
- Expect society to support you in the exercise of these rights

If you do not exercise your rights you will:
- Damage yourself psychologically
- Increase your levels of stress and anxiety
- Receive less than your fair share of those things you value
- Corrode and damage relationships with others

When you are responsibly assertive, you become your true self and encourage others to do the same.

BASIC ASSERTIVE RIGHTS

Every human has the right to:

- Be treated with respect
- Express opinions and feelings
- Set goals and objectives
- Refuse a request or say 'NO'
- Ask for what they want
- Make mistakes
- Be the judge of their own behaviour independent of the goodwill of others
- Get what they pay for
- Change their mind
- Decide whether or not to assert themselves

BASIC ASSERTIVE RIGHTS

To be treated with respect

- You have the right to live your life as you wish and pursue your own goals and objectives, providing you do no harm to others
- You have the right to be treated politely and courteously by others, irrespective of their position; dignity and respect are prerequisites of a civilised and democratic society

To express your opinions and feelings

- You have the right to express yourself
- Your view of situations and how you feel about them is as valuable as anyone else's
- If you wish to make your position or your emotions public then you have the right to do so; it is **you** not anyone else who decides whether or not you should

If we withhold our feelings and opinions others will not have the opportunity to know or understand us. Thus we will be denied the value and beauty of true friendship.

BASIC ASSERTIVE RIGHTS

To set your own goals and objectives

- You have the right to set your own goals
- Life is not a dress rehearsal; you don't have the luxury of a replay or extra time - this is it, and you are in control of what you want to do
- If you do not set your own agenda you will quickly find that you will be working to one set by others, who will not necessarily have your interests at heart

To refuse a request or say 'NO'

- You have the right to refuse
- When you are working to your own agenda and deciding what is and is not important, there will be a limited time for you to do what you want; when others make demands on your time you will have to decide whether or not you wish to give it
- Now and then you will want to say 'Yes' to yourself and 'No' to others - saying 'No' occasionally does not make you selfish; it makes you someone who is as concerned for yourself as you are for others

(39)

BASIC ASSERTIVE RIGHTS

To ask for what you want

- You have the right to express your own needs
- Each of us has needs, wants and desires and it is helpful in relationships to express them; first, it helps others give you what you really want and secondly, it also helps them ask for what they want
- You don't always get what you ask for, but will you get what you want if you do not ask?

To make mistakes

- You have the right to make mistakes
- Getting things wrong and making mistakes are essential parts of learning; we learn by our errors and we get things right by getting things wrong
- The only people who have not made mistakes are those who have done nothing with themselves or their lives

BASIC ASSERTIVE RIGHTS

To be the judge of your own behaviour independent of the goodwill of others

- You have the right to judge yourself; if we are people of worth and integrity we do not need other people to tell us what to do and what not to do
- You can judge your own behaviour, not needing the approbation or the criticism of others

To get what you pay for

- You have the right to get what you pay for; money is hard enough to gain without seeing it wasted on shoddy goods, workmanship or poor service
- You work hard for your money, what you receive in exchange for it should be of value
- If it is not, you have the right to demand the value, service or quality you have paid for, or be reimbursed

RIGHTS & RESPONSIBILITIES

BASIC ASSERTIVE RIGHTS

To change your mind

- You have the right to change your mind. Once, a very aggressive TV interviewer challenged a cabinet minister that at one time he was an active member of the Communist Party. After a few moments' reflection the Cabinet Minister replied "Yes, I was, and before that I used to believe in Father Christmas".
- To change is to grow and develop. If you challenge yourself, your ideas, your values, then change is inevitable.

To decide whether or not to assert yourself

- You have the right to choose for yourself.
- In any situation with others you can decide what is best for you and act accordingly. Sometimes this will mean that you will be assertive and say 'No' to something you would rather not do; and sometimes in the same situation you will say 'Yes', because you choose to please someone you love.
- The important point is that **you** make the choice, having reflected on the consequences and **taken responsibility** for the outcome.

OTHER BASIC RIGHTS

In programmes we have run, participants have decided upon a bill of rights for themselves. These have included the right to:

- State your limits and expectations
- Express your personal sexuality
- Make a statement not based on logic or rationality
- Make your own decisions
- Be independent of the company of others and enjoy 'me' time privacy
- Get involved in the affairs or problems of another or not
- Be ignorant and not understand
- Be successful
- Say 'I don't know'
- Ask for clarification when you don't understand

In working and thinking your way through this book and applying it to your own situation, you will gradually develop your own 'Bill of Rights'.

OTHER BASIC RIGHTS

THE FULCRUM OF ASSERTIVENESS

By exercising your rights, you are not demanding more than you deserve but expecting to be accorded what is justly yours. You are prepared to accept the outcomes of your actions in a responsible manner.

However, if you accept that you have rights and can exercise them, then you also automatically accept the responsibilities that flow from the benefits of those rights.

44

RESPONSIBILITIES

Definition: Being accountable for one's actions and decisions.

Just as we have rights so do other people, and just as we expect to have our rights respected and recognised we must do the same for others.

Nothing is free; for every personal action there is a social reaction or implication. When we choose to exercise one of our rights we must take responsibility for the outcome of that decision.

So, for example, you have the right to ask for what you want but you have responsibility to accept the consequences if someone says 'no' to your request. Similarly, if you say 'no' to a request then how that affects your relationship with the person you refuse is your responsibility.

CORRESPONDING RESPONSIBILITIES

RIGHT

I have the right to:

Be treated with respect

Express opinions and feelings

Set my own goals

Refuse a request or say 'no'

Ask for what I want

RESPONSIBILITY

Consequently my responsibility is to:

Respect the rights of others

Welcome the opinions and feelings of others

Help others to work to their goals and objectives

Encourage others to use their time in the way that they want

Encourage others to fulfil their needs

CORRESPONDING RESPONSIBILITIES

RIGHT

I have the right to:

Make mistakes

Express my sexuality

Get what I pay for

Change my mind

Decide whether or not to
assert myself

RESPONSIBILITY

Consequently my responsibility is to:

Help others learn through their mistakes
so that they can grow

Recognise sexual needs which may be
different from my own

Give best value and service for the money
and rewards I receive from others

Help others reach conclusions about their
experiences of the world

Allow others the freedom to choose how
they behave

RIGHTS AT WORK

As well as rights in life, there are rights at work. Basically there are three categories: statutory, organisational and personal.

Statutory Employee Rights

- To enjoy an equal opportunity to compete for work
- To be safe at work
- Not to be discriminated against at work
- To be paid in legal currency
- To have a contract of employment or service
- To be disciplined fairly
- Not to be dismissed arbitrarily
- To have your interests represented by another

RIGHTS & RESPONSIBILITIES

RIGHTS AT WORK

Organisational Employee Rights

- To be trained for what you do
- To be appraised regularly
- To know what is expected of you

Personal Employee Rights

- To be treated with respect
- To be consulted about those aspects of work that affect you
- To express your views about your work and how it is done
- To seek improvements in pay and conditions

Sometimes statutory obligations will override organisational and personal rights.
For instance, the organisation and you yourself might be willing to undertake unsafe
work practice for increased pay. However, statutory obligations will prevent this.
Sometimes organisational rights will override personal rights.

RIGHTS AT WORK

DEALING WITH CHALLENGES

1. Check your statutory rights; contact ACAS or The Health and Safety Commission.
2. Check organisational policies.
3. Check on previous precedents arising from similar instances which have occurred in the past.
4. Check with employers' organisations on what is best/good practice.
5. Check with Trade Union on what is best/good practice.
6. Present your findings and your request to management.
7. If you feel dissatisfied use the appeals system.
8. If appropriate, seek the assistance of an appropriate third party:
   - ACAS Officer
   - Health and Safety Officer or Rep
   - Trade Union Official.

RESPONSIBILITIES AT WORK

Responsibilities also mirror basic rights at work. Here are just some of them:

- To give of your best
- To attend work at agreed times
- To act safely
- To co-operate with reasonable management instructions
- To follow organisational policies, procedures and rules
- To use tools, equipment and resources correctly
- To co-operate with work colleagues
- To maintain agreed quality standards and procedures
- To promote your employer's legitimate commercial interests

Responsibilities such as these can be reasonably expected of you at work and you can reasonably expect them of your managers, colleagues and subordinates.

ASSERTIVENESS SKILLS

BODY LANGUAGE

Albert Mehrabian, a sociolinguist, suggested that the most impact from what we say comes from our body language. As can be seen from Mehrabian's pie chart below, when we are deciding whether or not someone means what they say 55% of the decision is influenced by body language and only 7% by what is said!!

Voice   **38%**

What is said   **7%**

Body Language   **55%**

Consequently, if you are going to
be assertive it is imperative that the words
that you say are matched by your body language.

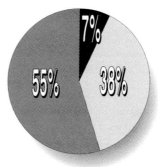

ASSERTIVENESS SKILLS

NON-ASSERTIVE BODY LANGUAGE

Posture:

- Bent
- Slumped
- Crooked

Facial Expression:

- Blank
- Half smiling in agreement
- Uninterested
- Afraid

Eyes:

- Looking down
- Minimum eye contact

Speech and Voice:

- Quiet
- Hesitant/Slow
- Weak
- Quick (when afraid or anxious)

Gestures:

- Restless
- Nodding head in agreement
- Pinching flesh
- Wringing hands

AGGRESSIVE BODY LANGUAGE

Posture:

- Rigid
- Tight fists
- Clenched teeth

Facial Expression:

- Tight jaw
- Glancing
- Frowning
- Eyes squinting
- Tense

Eyes:

- Staring
- Bulging
- Glazed over

Speech and Voice:

- Fast
- Loud
- Clipped
- High pitched
- Demanding
- Opinionated

Gestures:

- Pointing
- Finger wagging
- Finger stabbing
- Invading personal space
- Tense

ASSERTIVE BODY LANGUAGE

Posture:

- Upright
- Relaxed
- Open

Facial Expression:

- Committed
- Concerned
- Interested
- Responsive

Eyes:

- High eye contact

Speech and Voice:

- Direct
- Relaxed
- Friendly
- Well moderated
- Not strained

Gestures:

- Open
- Hands not raised above elbow
- Parallel shoulders

ASSERTIVENESS SKILLS

HANDLING CRITICISM

Criticism is useful because it provides feedback on the effects of your behaviour, and you can decide on whether or not it is beneficial to you. Sometimes criticism is malicious, unjustified or just plain wrong. Here is a basic procedure or checklist to help you deal with it.

1. Is the person qualified to make the criticism; do they know you well enough?

2. Is the behaviour being criticised something it is possible for you to change? (Remember, it is almost impossible for you to change your personality. If you are naturally 'shy' or 'independent' that is the way you are and the other person will have to accept it. You can only change your behaviour).

3. Are you conscious that you do what is being criticised? If not, monitor yourself as to how often and in what circumstances the behaviour occurs.

HANDLING CRITICISM

4. Does your criticised behaviour occur frequently enough to warrant your attention?
5. Are the results of your criticised behaviour significant enough to warrant your attention?
6. Reflect on why you might behave in that way - what benefits or disadvantages might there be for you in continuing with it?
7. Think whether or not you wish to change your behaviour; what would be the advantages to you?
8. Make the decision whether or not to change, and act on your decision.

ASSERTIVENESS SKILLS

DEALING WITH CRITICISM

Deal with criticism rationally and logically, not emotionally. Here are some hints:

● Criticism is only feedback; it is about your **behaviour**, not you as a person

● Some criticism is unfounded; so all criticism needs to be verified to discover what is useful and what is not

● It is inappropriate to extrapolate criticisms - it is unwise to generate from specifics

● Criticisms should be **thought** through not **fought** through

● If the criticism is not about specific behaviour then it is of little or no value

ASSERTIVENESS SKILLS

GIVING CRITICISM

Should you feel the need to criticise others, then treat them in the way you would
like to be treated.

- Only criticise behaviour the person can change
- Be as specific as you can
- Be able to give other examples of similar behaviour by the other person
- Make the criticism as soon after the 'behaviour' as possible; otherwise it will not be
  helpful - do not be drawn into 'and another thing' accusations
- Use a matter of fact voice and keep your body language positive
- Use empathetic statements: - 'This might be difficult for you ...'
  - 'You may not be aware ...'
  - 'This may come as a surprise ...'
  - 'It is not going to be easy for you to deal with this ...'

- Recognise and reward the   - 'Thank you for listening to me ...'
  person, eg: - 'I'm sure you won't do that again ...'
  - 'I'm confident you can do better ...'

RESPONDING TO CRITICISM

You cannot escape criticism, so it is sensible and healthy to accept it and work through it. It may help to remember that:

- Not all criticism is useful
- Not all criticism is fair
- Not all criticism is justified
- Not all criticism is correct

but being assertive helps you
deal with criticism effectively.

Non-assertive people when criticised
ingratiate themselves, stay quiet and appear to accept it.
Internally, though, they may be fuming, hurting or perhaps wanting further explanation.

RESPONDING TO CRITICISM

Some people accept all criticism as automatically true, and attempt to change themselves to please others. This is dangerous, especially if the criticism is unjustified and/or incorrect.

Aggressive people will immediately attack or go to great lengths to justify their behaviour.

Being assertive means that you can accept and work with criticism. You know that with feedback you are able to understand fully the implications and effects of your behaviour.

Assertive people can: deal with criticism
give criticism

without being emotional, and without it affecting their dignity or integrity as individuals.

RECEIVING POSITIVE FEEDBACK

Frequently we discount compliments and genuine positive feedback:

'It was nothing really .....'
'Anyone could do it .....'

In doing so not only are WE rejecting valuable information about ourselves, but we are also punishing the giver. If we continually discount compliments we will be training family and friends not to give them, thus condemning ourselves to live in the gloomy world of continual criticism.

Compliments are the gold trading stamps of friends, and build the self-esteem of both giver and recipient.

Receiving compliments is so easy. All it takes is a smile - which is, after all, the best thing you can do with your face - and the words 'thank you'.

Once you become comfortable with receiving compliments, you will find it easier to give them. Life is too short not to tell people how they please you or what you like about them.

POSITIVE FEEDBACK

When you accept a courtesy:

- Your ego is boosted
- You feel better about yourself
- You appear more confident
- You will receive compliments more frequently
- Those who compliment you feel good

When you give positive feedback, people:

- Feel good about themselves
- Have their self-esteem boosted
- Feel more motivated and committed
- Appreciate and respect you more
- Work better with others
- Improve their performance

(65)

ASSERTIVENESS SKILLS

HOW TO DISAGREE

Being assertive means having your own views. Since others will also have their views, this means that occasionally there will be disagreements. Acquiescing or, the opposite, attacking, are not constructive responses.

Following a simple step-by-step process will help you put your case without **getting emotional, losing your integrity or losing your respect for the other person.**

The Process

1. Affirmative Statement
2. Softening Statement
3. Indicate Process
4. State Reasons
5. Disagree
6. Offer a compromise*

* The compromise is optional and it is for you to decide whether or not to make a concession.

DISAGREEMENT PROCESS

1. The Affirmative Statement

This is simply saying 'YES'. It might sound strange saying this when you are disagreeing. But if you say 'NO' the other person immediately goes into argument mode and is less likely to listen. You are using 'yes' to prepare them for what you are going to say, not to indicate that you agree with them.

2. The Softening Statement

Most people's views are influenced by their background, experience or profession. You can show that you recognise this within the context of a softening statement. Here are some examples:-

- 'As an engineer I can understand why you take such a position'
- 'As someone much older than myself, with different values, I can understand where you come from'
- 'As a man working in a traditional male environment and culture I can understand why you said that'
- 'As a manager whose prime responsibility is for output I can understand your position makes a great deal of sense'

DISAGREEMENT PROCESS

3. Indicate Process
This explains to the person the process you will use to outline your position or your reasons for the stance that you have taken. Here are some examples:

- 'If I may, I would like to say something about that ...'
- 'Let me give you my reasons'
- 'Can I tell you how I have arrived at my viewpoint ...?'
- 'Let me outline briefly my position and the reasons for it ...'

If there is going to be any sensible discussion, the other person has to let you put your case. If they are not prepared to listen then you are wasting your time anyway, and it would be better to terminate the discussion immediately.

4. State Reasons
Here you simply give the reasons or justification for your position. This can either be done in a straightforward way, or you can give a balanced view of pros and cons, explaining why you have come down on the side that you have.

DISAGREEMENT PROCESS

5. Disagree
Do not apologise or use tentative language here. Use the strongest language that you can, remembering to accompany what you have said with appropriate body language. Here are some examples:

- 'So I cannot agree with you'
- 'So I must disagree'
- 'So I think you are mistaken'

The two letters of the adverb 'so' are exceptionally powerful because they make your conclusions 'so' logical and natural.

6. Compromise
This is optional, but helpful if there is little or no cost to you. However, your compromise should always be conditional on your getting what you want (see examples).

DISAGREEMENT PROCESS

EXAMPLES

Position: 'I don't think you should go out tonight'

Affirmative	1.	'Yes'
Softening	2.	'I can quite understand why you would like me to stay in and keep you company as I have done the last three Saturdays'
Indicate	3.	'Let me explain why tonight is so important to me'
State	4.	'I particularly want to see this production of Macbeth because it has had excellent reviews and if I don't see it tonight I will miss it'
Disagree	5.	'So I have decided that I am going to go out'
Compromise	6.	'But I am more than happy to keep you company tomorrow.'

DISAGREEMENT PROCESS

EXAMPLES

Position: 'I want you to work overtime tonight'

Affirmative	1.	'Yes, I can understand that'
Softening	2.	'We have been short staffed all week and I know it has been difficult'
Indicate	3.	'But I have to tell you something'
State	4.	'I have not seen my children very much this week and tonight I promised to take them to the park'
Disagree	5.	'So I cannot work overtime tonight'
Compromise	6.	'Would it be helpful if I stayed tomorrow?'

Position: 'You can't have an increase in salary'

Affirmative	1.	'Yes, it must be difficult'
Softening	2.	'I know that business has not been good these last 6 months'
Indicate	3.	'But my position is this'
State	4.	'I was promised a raise within 3 months of starting and that was deferred; I have now been here 12 months, and besides doing good work, you have increased my responsibilities considerably'
Disagree	5.	'So it is important that I get the pay rise due to me. Thank you.'

'I' STATEMENTS

'I' statements are among the most powerful you can make, both for yourself and others.

In 'I' statements you are affirming who you are and what you want. Using them is the hallmark of assertiveness.

'I' statements can be used in a variety of ways:

- Situation
- Interpretation and understanding
- Feelings and emotions
- Wants and needs
- Future actions

ASSERTIVENESS SKILLS

'I' STATEMENTS

Situation

- 'I have been asked to work late three times this week'
- 'I see that I have been passed over for promotion again'
- 'I notice that you have not spoken to me for three days'

Situation statements are powerful because they are factual and, as an observation on your part, they are non-negotiable. They describe the world as you see it and the way it affects you directly.

Interpretation and Understanding

- 'I get the impression you are not interested'
- 'I have the feeling you don't want my ideas'
- 'I think you are ignoring me'

These statements are powerful because you're describing your interpretation of a situation, not just the situation itself. It tells the other person directly the effect their behaviour is having on you.

ASSERTIVENESS SKILLS

'I' STATEMENTS

Feelings and Emotions

- 'I feel betrayed'
- 'I feel taken advantage of'
- 'I feel angry, disappointed, cross, annoyed'

This is not about feelings, but really a way to express your opinion more strongly. Again, these statements are powerful because they are non-negotiable or irrefutable. No one can challenge you and say 'No, you don't feel that way'.

Wants and Needs

- 'I want you to pay attention'
- 'I want your full co-operation'
- 'I want you to be on time'

The strength of these statements is that they let the other person know your exact position and what you expect. They don't have to guess. They can only say 'Yes', 'No' or negotiate.

ASSERTIVENESS SKILLS

'I' STATEMENTS

Future Actions

- 'I will remind you every Monday'
- 'I will ensure that I am available to talk to you'
- 'I will report you next time it happens'

The other person knows what will happen next,
so there are no surprises.

PUTTING THE 'I's TOGETHER

It is now possible to put together 'I' combinations. When you decide to be assertive 'I' combinations are very powerful.

Situation: 'I see that this is the third time you have not done as I requested'

Interpretation: 'I think you are trying to do as little as possible when I am not with you'

Feelings: 'I feel disappointed and annoyed that I have to repeat myself'

Want: 'So I want you to do what I ask even if I'm not there to supervise you'

Future Action: 'I am going to report you if you do this again'

HOW TO GIVE ASSERTIVE INSTRUCTIONS
(ASKING FOR WHAT YOU WANT)

Much of management, and indeed parenthood, is about asking people for what you want. Some of us were taught as children that it was rude to ask for things. It is as if you hope that others have a crystal ball, so that they will know how to please you.

Sometimes we play games or make excuses for people:
- 'They should know by now'
- 'It is obvious what is required'
- 'If they had any sense they would know'

The process or structure of asking for what you want is very simple.
The components are:
- The person's name
- What you want
- Why you want it
- When you want it
    plus
- The assumptive 'thank you'

ASKING FOR WHAT YOU WANT

'Peter,
I would like you to transfer to line 10 as from tomorrow, because they are short staffed and it will be good for your cross training.
Thank you.'

'Mary,
Will you complete that report before you go home tonight so that I can have it for the Management Meeting first thing tomorrow.
Thank you.'

Remember: Instructions must be given with the appropriate body language to have their full impact. (See page 54)

ASSERTIVENESS SKILLS

BROKEN RECORD

When a record gets stuck it plays the same thing over and over again. So, in *broken record* all you have to do is to repeat yourself again and again and again, until the person gives in or concedes to your demands.

Children are masters at *broken record,* but somehow during adolescence we lose the skill. In my experience most people capitulate after you repeat yourself three times.

Broken record is particularly useful when:
- Dealing with those in authority, or when you feel that the other person has more expertise than you
- You think you are not getting what you are entitled to
- You are dealing with people brighter or more fluent than you
- The other person is likely to use put-downs, or attack you verbally

Because you just have to repeat yourself, *broken record* is really easy to use.

BROKEN RECORD EXAMPLES

Example 1

You: 'The programme was not up to standard, and we did not cover all the elements promised in the brochure so I want a refund.'

Reply: *'Other people have not complained, in fact some of the evaluations are excellent.'*

You: 'They might be, but I want a refund because the work was not up to standard.'

Reply: *'In my opinion as a course tutor the course was up to standard.'*

You: 'I can appreciate that is your opinion but I want a refund.'

Reply: *'It is not our policy to give refunds.'*

You: 'That may be your policy but I want a refund.'

BROKEN RECORD EXAMPLES

Example 2

You:	'I'm not satisfied with the service, I would like to see the manager.'
Reply:	*'He is busy right now.'*
You:	'I'm sure he is, but I would still like to see him.'
Reply:	*'He doesn't usually get involved in these matters.'*
You:	'I can understand that, but I want to see him.'
Reply:	*'You will have to make an appointment and write in.'*
You:	'That may be your procedure, but I want to see him now.'
Reply:	*'Well, if you would like to wait for an hour I'll see what I can do.'*
You:	'Thank you but I want to see him now.'

And on...
    and on...
        and on...
            and on...

NEGATIVE ASSERTION

When people call us names, or give us negative labels, we usually wish to defend ourselves, or feel so hurt that we retreat. Aggressive or manipulative people who do this to us soon find our weak spots. They use them to make us do what they want or to score points off us.

Negative assertion is like jujitsu where you use the power of your protagonist to turn the situation to your advantage. No one is perfect, so in negative assertion all you do is accept the part of the statement, name or label that is true, in a matter of fact way. Look at the examples:

> *'If you think that, you must be stupid'*

You: 'I admit I'm not the brightest person around'

> *'And you are always making mistakes'*

You: 'Yes, I do make mistakes occasionally'

> *'And you are lazy'*

You: 'I never claim to be the hardest working person'

ASSERTIVENESS SKILLS

FOGGING

Fogging is useful when someone is putting pressure on you to do something that is really not in your best interest, and you would rather not do it. Thus your response to the request is to put up a fog.

Listen to what the person says, and decide whether or not you wish to comply. If not, then using their words, or similar, acknowledge their need but state your case. In this way you show the person that you have understood their request, but that you are not going to comply. This method is a very polite method of saying 'No'.

REQUEST	RESPONSE
'I want it now'	'I can see why you would want that but my priority is ....'
'You should help me'	'Perhaps I should but right now I have other priorities.'
'This is important'	'Of course it is important but not as important as ....'
'I need this'	'I am sure you do but it is just not possible now.'

By using this technique you are less likely to be manipulated into doing something you would rather not and yet you cannot be accused of recognising the other person's need.

NEGATIVE ENQUIRY

Once you have mastered Negative Assertion and Fogging you will be ready for Negative Enquiry, which is real fun. Here you invite extra criticism and/or examples so that you have the benefit of additional feedback.

ACCUSATION

'You're lazy'   'Oh really, in what way specifically?'

'You're always late'   'Always? How do you know that for a fact?'

'You're stupid'   'My understanding may be different from yours, what exactly do you mean by that?'

'You're selfish'   'Can you explain why this particular instance has caused you to brand me with such a label?'

If the person is genuine and cares for you, such replies will lead to real feedback. Then you can decide whether the accusation is justified, and whether you want to do anything about it (see page 58 onwards).

POWER WORDS

In being assertive certain words are very powerful indeed and used in the correct context are exceptionally persuasive.

Power words and phrases are:

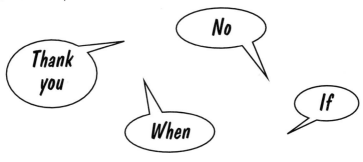

ASSERTIVENESS SKILLS

NO

'No' is one of the most difficult words to say to another person. This is usually because we fear the loss of their goodwill or regard.

We naturally wish to be thought of as kind, helpful, considerate people. It makes us feel good to please others, so in the short term it is easier to say 'yes' than say 'no'.

Here is a checklist for when you want to say `NO':

1. Do I really want this or am I pleasing someone else?
2. What is the benefit to me of saying 'yes'?
3. If I do it will I enjoy it?
4. Do I have to say 'yes' or 'no' right now; is it to my advantage to delay my decision?
5. How do I feel about the request? How do I feel emotionally about it?
6. Do I need more information before I make my decision?
7. Do I want an alternative?
8. What is the cost of saying 'no'?

The checklist is a long one so you can always use number four to give yourself some thinking time (and go back to this list).

ASSERTIVENESS SKILLS

HOW TO SAY NO

- Just say 'no'
  Do not preface it with an 'I'm sorry but ...'
  or tentative language 'I would really
  like to but ...'

- Give an explanation of your feelings:
  'It does not feel right to ...'
  'I don't like to ...'
  'I would feel compromised to ...'

- Give an explanation of your reasons:
  'Because I must do such and such'
  'Because I am already committed'
  'Because I don't have the time'

- If appropriate thank the person:
  'Thank you for thinking of me'
  'Thank you for the invitation'

ASSERTIVENESS SKILLS

THANK YOU

'Thank you' is an interesting phrase. We are brought up to say 'please' when we want something. But, if we say 'please' we are asking the person for something. Consequently, they have the initiative because they can say 'yes' or 'no'.

We are taught to say 'thank you' when we have been given something that we have requested. But something interesting happens when we say 'thank you' where we would normally say 'please'. The 'thank you' becomes assumptive. In other words you assume that what you ask for will be done or given.

Used with appropriate assertive body language the judicial use of 'thank you' can be exceptionally powerful.

- 'I would like to be quiet now. Thank you.'
- 'I would like you to help me. Thank you.'
- 'I want you to pay attention. Thank you.'

ASSERTIVENESS SKILLS

IF

The conjunction 'if' is exceptionally powerful when you want to make a concession or give something away. The 'if' acts as a piece of elastic with which you can pull back the concession, if you don't get what you want.

'If' becomes conditional:
- 'If you do this then I will ...'
- 'If you work harder I will ...'
- 'If you co-operate you can have ...'

Most grandmothers know this because of Grandma's Law of Vitamin Intake for Children, which goes:
'If you eat your vegetables you can have your pudding.'

Notice how a low priority option is coupled with a high priority choice.
In life most of us let people have the 'pudding' first, hoping that they will do the decent thing and give us what we want. If only life was that simple!

WHEN

This is another conjunction which is the same as `if' when you make it conditional. It has the same power:

- 'When you ...'
- 'When the work has been completed ...'
- 'When you stop making accusations ...'

ASSERTIVE ACTIVITIES

ASSERTIVE ACTIVITIES

GENERAL ADVICE

Before you start on the activities here is some advice to assist you in your progress to become more assertive.

1. Expect surprise and even opposition
It has taken a lifetime to get you to behave the way you do now, so do not expect to change overnight. Also remember that those who are close to you will not expect your behaviour to change. There may be others who have a vested interest in keeping you non-assertive or aggressive.

This means that when you decide to change your behaviour, as well as disciplining yourself, you must also expect surprise, even opposition, from others who know and have a vested interest in the 'old you'.

2. 'By the inch it's a cinch but by the yard it is very hard'
It is unwise to set yourself too ambitious targets - start with acorns and let them grow slowly into oaks. Go for small increments of change and build on them.

GENERAL ADVICE

3. Expect failure and use it

Failure is part of change. When you try anything new, but especially behaviour, it is unlikely that you will get it right first time. You get it wrong before you get it right. Be both realistic and resilient when you fail. 'If at first you don't succeed, try harder'.

Remember, success only comes before work in a dictionary!!

4. Allow for slippage

When you squeeze a ball you create an indentation, but when you stop the ball reverts to its original shape. Human behaviour is just like that ball - it will revert to its old comfortable ways. So expect slippage, but do not give in to it.

GENERAL ADVICE

5. It takes time

Behaviour changes slowly. Crash diets or crash exercises do not work; nor do crash behaviour changes. Just think about the simple skill of learning to drive, with the hours of instruction and practice it requires. To become assertive takes just as much time and effort, perhaps even more.

Remember

> **THOUGHTS** lead to
> > **ACTIONS** which lead to
> > > **HABITS** which lead to
> > > > **CHARACTER** which leads to
> > > > > **PERSONALITY** which leads to
> > > > > > **THE NEW YOU**

Just as for smokers the body fights against giving up nicotine, so your present mindset will resist you making changes. It will take time for you to settle down to the new assertive you.

94

ASSERTIVE ACTIVITIES

GENERAL ADVICE

6. **Set SMART goals**

S	- Specific	- define exactly what you want
M	- Measurable	- what will be the success criteria
A	- Appropriate	- ensure they are appropriate for you
R	- Realistic	- they must be feasible
T	- Timebound	- by when are you going to do it

Goals are dreams that you are going to make real. They are not miracles - you won't be the first person to fly by flapping your arms. If you weren't born in America you cannot be President. If you're 55 you are not likely to be an Olympic swimmer. But you can easily be assertive by:

- Stating what you want
- Stating your limits
- Saying 'No'
- Getting what you pay for
- Demanding respect
- Changing your mind
- Giving a speech or a presentation

Most people find committing their goals to writing very helpful.

Tip: Keep a log book or journal where you record your thoughts, objectives, goals and learning points. It is good discipline and will help you marshal your thoughts, and be more specific and focused. It is also very motivating to look back and see what you have achieved.

ASSERTIVE ACTIVITIES

KEY POINTS FOR ASSERTIVENESS

1. Genetics ain't fair - physically or intellectually you can only go with what you've got.
2. No one can do it for you - you have to do it for yourself.
3. If you don't decide for yourself about your life, someone else will decide for you.
4. This is it, there is no second chance this time around.
5. The longer you don't use it the quicker you lose it.
6. Life is a learning experience - you cannot fail, you can only choose.
7. The most important thing you can do is to choose, the worst thing you can do is not pursue your choice.
8. Nothing is free - good things take time and they come in very thin slices.
9. You are your biggest asset and your best resource.
10. You know all that you need to know to do what you have to do.

**"The more you do of what you're doing the
more you'll get of what you've got."**

ASSERTIVE ACTIVITIES

ACTIVITY NO. 1
PERSONAL RECORD

Have a log book and in it keep:

- Quotations that inspire you
- Your basic rights
- A list of your personal goals and ambitions
- A list of your fantasies and dreams
- Your affirmations
- A list of your achievements
  - personal
  - family
  - work
  - community
- A list of your personal bests

READ IT AND UPDATE IT REGULARLY.

ASSERTIVE ACTIVITIES

ACTIVITY NO. 2

HEROES

Read biographies of people that you admire - your heroes and heroines.

In what way are you similar to them in terms of:

- Background
- Personality
- Attitudes
- Values

Construct a list of their values from your reading, and see which of them you could make your own.

What do you think their personal affirmations would be? Make a list and see which of them you could make your own.

When faced with a difficult situation, think how your hero or heroine would deal with the matter, and act accordingly.

ASSERTIVE ACTIVITIES

ACTIVITY NO. 3

SCRIPTS

Remember, when you see a good film or play, that behind each scene there has been a considerable amount of rehearsing. Sometimes a two minute scene in a film takes days to get right. Apply the technique to yourself in your new assertive role.

1. Think what you want from a situation.
2. Script out what you are going to say.
3. Learn your script.
4. Practise your script verbally.
5. Practise your script with appropriate body language.
6. Decide on the best time, place and person for you to use this behaviour.
7. DO IT.
8. Reward yourself for trying, and learn from the experience for improvements next time.

ACTIVITY NO. 4

CUSHION TALK

This is similar to Activity 3 and helps you practise. It is also useful for you to 'finish off' conversations that have had a significant emotional content for you. Recreate the original scene in your mind with the cushion as the person, regenerate the emotions that you felt at the time, and then when you are ready, talk to the cushion. It is good for purging emotions so that next time you can talk to the person using reason and avoid getting upset.

You can also try variations of words, themes and approaches to the assertive opportunity you have decided to act upon. You can play out the 'what ifs', so that you will be better prepared for the real situation.

Remember, however much you practise, in real situations there will always be unexpected variations, but your practice sessions will make you better prepared. Boxers skip and go on long runs wearing heavy boots; you see neither of these activities when they fight in the ring, but such exercises make them better prepared for the fight. Writing out and rehearsing what you want to say will help you in being assertive.

ASSERTIVE ACTIVITIES

ACTIVITY NO. 5
CHUNK IT DOWN

This relates back to Advice Point 2. If you are having special difficulty with a particular individual it may not be wise to go the whole assertive hog at once. It will be too much for you. In athletic terms it would be like attempting a marathon without practice or training. Not only will you fail, it will also be extremely painful for you.

For instance, if you are going to be assertive with a manager at work who intimidates you, chunk down your behaviour so that you build yourself up slowly.

1. Put yourself in their presence as often as you can - you don't have to say anything or behave differently from normal. *Then:*
2. Practise assertive body language with eye contact, body direction and space. Again, you don't have to say anything. *Then, when you are ready:*
3. When the person speaks, make summary statements of what they have said wherever appropriate, eg: 'So what you're saying is..., is that right?' *Then, when you are ready:*
4. Use the disagreement technique, suggested earlier (see page 66 onwards).

People that you find difficult are likely to be aggressive rather than assertive, so your new behaviour is going to take them by surprise. Expect an initial aggressive response and deal with it assertively.

ASSERTIVE ACTIVITIES

ACTIVITY NO. 6

GIVING COMPLIMENTS

- Make a list of five friends or colleagues; for each one, list three or four things that you like about them and think of examples when they demonstrate these qualities or behaviours.
- Script out what you will say to them when they next engage in the behaviour; use 'I' statements ('I think/feel/would like you to know' - rather than just 'You are so good at ...') and be specific, mentioning their actual behaviour in your praise.
- See how they respond and note whether or not they increase that behaviour when they are with you.
- For a week resolve to compliment at least three people for their work, behaviour or support they give you; make a note in your diary of your specific 'praises' to remind yourself that you have actually done it - it is not easy!
- Make a list of all the specific things you like about your wife, husband, partner, child. Plan a day ahead when you know they are not going to be working and then sit them down, tell them all the things you specifically like about them; as a reward give them a 'me' day when they can do what they like and you can spoil them. Why wait for Mother's Day, Father's Day or a birthday? Do it now!!

ASSERTIVE ACTIVITIES

ACTIVITY NO. 7

FIND A MENTOR

Select someone you know, who knows you well and whose views you respect. Tell them that you have put yourself on your own personal assertiveness programme and, because you hold them in high esteem, you would greatly appreciate it if they would be your occasional mentor.

Share with them, review and discuss:

- Your goals and objectives
- Your scripts
- Your successes and failures
- What you find difficult
- What you find easy

At the end of each meeting, agree objectives and what you are going to do next.

Tip: Space your meetings out by six to eight weeks to give sufficient time to practise, fail, learn and do again. Keep a log of your progress.

ASSERTIVE ACTIVITIES

ACTIVITY NO. 8
FEEDBACK & CRITICISM

- Select someone you know, who knows your behaviour well and whose views you respect. Tell them you have put yourself on your own personal assertiveness programme and, because you hold them in high esteem, you would really value their feedback and criticism.

- Agree a mutually agreeable time and place which can guarantee privacy, confidentiality and comfort.

- Several days before the meeting, send them the list below and ask them for specific feedback, with as many actual examples of your behaviour as possible.

- Agree confidentiality protocols.

   The list
   1. What is it about me that is attractive and why?
   2. What is it about me that is not attractive and why?
   3. What do you think about the way I dress and the image that I project?
   4. Where have I used my abilities to the full and where is there an opportunity to improve?
   5. Which of my personal habits annoy you and why?

ASSERTIVE ACTIVITIES

ACTIVITY NO. 8

FEEDBACK & CRITICISM

6. How confident do you think I am and why?
7. How assertive do you think I am and why?
8. What do you think of my interpersonal skills?
9. How can I get on better with people?
10. How fluent am I?
11. How do I show my emotions?
12. If you had only three adjectives to describe me, what would they be and why?
13. What should I do to improve my social skills?
14. What sort of partner, parent, friend, employee do you think I have been and what can I do to improve?
15. What would I have to change to improve my relations with you?

This information will be invaluable to you; accept it as it comes and do not attempt to justify yourself to your friend or to yourself.

- Work through this information with the criticism checklist given earlier in the book (see pages 58-59). Reflect, and select what aspect of the information you choose to work on.

ASSERTIVE ACTIVITIES

ACTIVITY NO. 9
AIDS TO SELF-ESTEEM

Much of assertiveness is linked to self-esteem and the views we hold of ourselves. You can significantly improve your psychological self-esteem by looking after yourself. These basic rules you know, so they are set out here to remind you and to encourage you to do something about it.

1. Get up or down to your ideal weight, given your body shape and bone structure.
2. Exercise regularly and get yourself physically fit.
3. Your body is what you eat, so eat sensibly.
4. Plan 'me' time so that part of every week you have time for yourself.
5. Replace television with an interest that will stretch you in some way - physically, socially, intellectually or emotionally.
6. Plan quality time with your family and those who are emotionally significant for you.
7. Reward yourself for your successes - small rewards for small things, significant rewards for major achievements.

ASSERTIVE ACTIVITIES

ACTIVITY NO. 10
ANY TIME, ANYWHERE!

Assertiveness can be practised anywhere at any time. Here are some ideas:

1. Spend a day a week on the way to work catching people's eyes and then holding their glance until:
   (a) they look away;
   (b) you smile and say 'good morning'.
2. Go to a market stall and haggle over the price by:
   (a) making them an offer;
   (b) asking if they can do it cheaper.
3. Use assumptive language on your family and friends and monitor the results.

The Management Pocketbook Series

About the Author

Max A. Eggert is an international management psychologist who specialises in assisting organisations and individuals to achieve their best. He works mainly in the UK and Australia. A respected authority on the human and organisational aspects of change and empowerment, Max has delivered workshops and seminars to thousands of executives and managers throughout the world.

Other books by Max A. Eggert include:
The Managing Your Appraisal Pocketbook; The Management and Delivery of Outplacement; The Perfect CV (in top 10 business books); The Perfect Interview; The Perfect Career; The Perfect Consultant; Career Questions.

He can be contacted in Australia at:
Interim, Level 16, Norwich House, 6-10 O'Connell Street, Sydney, NSW 2000, Australia.
Tel: (02) 9223 2388   Fax: (02) 9223 2331

and in Britain at:
94 High Street, Lindfield, Sussex RH16 2HP, England.
Tel: (0144) 448 3057   Fax: (0144) 448 4867

© 1997 Max A. Eggert

Published in 1997 by Management Pocketbooks Ltd   ISBN 1 870471 45 8
14 East Street, Alresford, Hants SO24 9EE

Printed in England by Alresford Press Ltd

ORDER FORM

Your details	Please send me:	No. copies

Your details

Name _____

Position _____

Company _____

Address _____

_____

_____

Telephone _____

Facsimile _____

VAT No. (EC companies) _____

Your Order Ref _____

Please send me:

The Assertiveness _____ Pocketbook ☐

The _____ Pocketbook ☐

The _____ Pocketbook ☐

The _____ Pocketbook ☐

The _____ Pocketbook ☐

The _____ Pocketbook ☐

The _____ Pocketbook ☐

**MANAGEMENT
POCKETBOOKS**

14 EAST STREET ALRESFORD
HAMPSHIRE SO24 9EE
Tel: (01962) 735573
Fax: (01962) 733637